foreword

## Foreword

*Up Close* has been published to celebrate the re-opening of Manchester Art Gallery in 2002, following the completion of a four-year refurbishment and expansion programme. Comprising the construction of a new wing designed by Michael Hopkins & Partners, linking together the Royal Manchester Institution and the Athenaeum buildings (previously housing the Art Gallery), this £35 million project has realised a century-old ambition to expand the Art Gallery, creating a world class facility which will open in the year the city hosts the Commonwealth Games. The project has been made possible by major grants from the Heritage Lottery Fund, the European Regional Development Fund, the generous commitment of the City Council and many benefactors, both private and corporate.

The city's collections are part of Manchester's and the nation's heritage. Some of the most important works in the collections were gifted to us, either from private collections or by the Contemporary Art Society. Others were purchased by the City Council. Recent acquisitions have been made with the generous support of The Friends of Manchester City Galleries, the Corporate Patrons of Manchester City Galleries, the Heritage Lottery Fund, the National Art Collections Fund, and the Government Purchase Grant Fund administered by the Victoria and Albert Museum. We have also benefited from purchases made under the auspices of the C.A.S. Special Collection Scheme, with funds from the Arts Council Lottery Fund, the Corporate Patrons and the Crafts Council.

This book provides an introduction to these collections, which are characterised by an extraordinary diversity, ranging from our world famous collection of Pre-Raphaelite paintings, English earthenware and eighteenth-century silver, to an unrivalled collection of British art from the mid-nineteenth century to the mid-twentieth century. There is also a distinguished collection of Dutch seventeenth-century pictures, a growing group of twentieth-century decorative art and an important collection of works on paper which until now has been rarely exhibited.

In devising this book we worked with Michael Howard, practising artist and Senior Lecturer in History of Art at the Manchester Metropolitan University, to capture something of the unique flavour of the collections, whilst also including his personal favourites. We deliberately avoided a thematic or chronological approach, allowing the images to create their own narrative, and we hope that his enthusiasm and insight will inspire visitors to explore the rich collections of the Gallery.

We are delighted that Manchester Metropolitan University, through Professor Roger Wilson (Dean of the Faculty of Art and Design), has contributed towards the production of this publication, in recognition of the strong historical links between both institutions. The city's first School of Design was established in the original Art Gallery building in 1838 as part of the Royal Manchester Institution.

**Cllr Glynn Evans**
Executive Member for Culture and Leisure

**Virginia Tandy**
Director of Manchester City Galleries

## Introduction

The great Victorian city galleries developed from the private cabinets of curiosities that were established by the kings, princes and merchants of the Renaissance. They are places at once wonderful, extraordinary, bizarre and contradictory – compelling and exhausting in turns. In an age when the distinctions that separate shopping malls from cathedrals and restaurants from museums are becoming increasingly blurred, it is worthwhile considering the exact nature of this familiar institution. As well as being somewhere to shelter from the weather, to take the children, to meet parents, friends or lovers, or to buy a postcard, T-shirt or tea towel, it is above all a place in which certain valued artefacts are stored, kept safe and offered in a sympathetic setting for consideration and contemplation. Separated from the noise and rush of the city, the gallery offers a place open to all, specifically designed for education, reflection, meditation and, not least, pleasure. Once inside, visitors are encouraged to enter into an active conversation with the works of art to be found there and, through that engagement, to ask questions of themselves, of others and of the world around them.

In the late eighteenth century Manchester developed from being a small market town to becoming, within a few decades, the first modern industrial city and the world's leading producer and exporter of cotton goods. The wealthy and influential businessmen of the city created, just as their counterparts in Renaissance Italy had done 300 years earlier, institutions that would not only serve the community but would give Manchester a sense of identity and purpose. Celebrated and castigated in equal measure as a place of manufacture and commerce, the city had a need to show the world that it was also a centre of culture and taste.

Throughout the Victorian period and into our own unsettled times, it has generally been held that exposure to great works of art has a moral effect upon the beholder. In a parliamentary speech made in 1832 in support of the building of the National Gallery, Sir Robert Peel gave voice to a common understanding that, 'the exacerbation of angry and unsocial feelings might be much softened by the effects which the fine arts have ever produced on the minds of men.' In Manchester, as elsewhere, many of the collectors who donated works of art to the Gallery did so believing that their actions would not only ameliorate the lot of the common people but would also strengthen their moral fibre, and thereby lessen the possibility of social discontent and, accordingly, improve productivity.

Support for a 'Manchester Institution for the Promotion of Literature, Science and the Arts' was widespread and in January 1824, less than a year after the project had been initiated, the impressive sum of £23,000 had been raised by public subscription. A competition followed to find a suitable design for what was referred to as Manchester's 'temple to the arts'. The successful submission came from Charles Barry who would later find fame and a knighthood as the architect of the Houses of Parliament. His austere and symmetrical design, in the newly fashionable Greek Revival style, clearly articulated the city's cultural ambitions and implicitly suggested a political equation between the democratic independent

*Opposite:*
Manchester Art Gallery, past and present: J.W. Hart's watercolour of the interior hall of the Royal Manchester Institution (exh. 1838), view of Barry's facade, and the new build by Michael Hopkins & Partners.

upclose

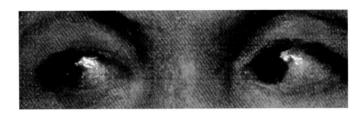

A Guide to
MANCHESTER ART GALLERY

Michael Howard

SCALA

Text and photography © Manchester City Galleries, 2002

First published in 2002 by Scala Publishers Ltd
Gloucester Mansions
140a Shaftesbury Avenue
London WC2H 8HD

Edited by Victoria Poskitt
Designed by Yvonne Dedman

ISBN I 85759 2794

*Up Close* is published with the generous support of
Manchester City Galleries Development Trust

Manchester City Galleries

www.manchestergalleries.org

*Cover (front):*
**Autumn Leaves** (detail) 1855–56,
by Sir John Millais (see page 50)

*Cover (back):*
**Queen Pineapple** (detail) 1994–95,
by Kate Malone (see page 27)

*Title page:*
**Othello, the Moor of Venice** (detail) 1826,
by James Northcote (see page 6)

*Right:*
**Albert Square, Manchester** (detail) 1910,
by Adolphe Valette (see page 73)

*Othello, the Moor of Venice* 1826
James Northcote (1746–1831)
Oil on canvas, 76.2 x 63.5 cm

It has been suggested that the purchase of this painting was prompted by Manchester being at the centre of the anti-slavery movement. This was the gallery's first purchase, acquired for 30 guineas from the first exhibition of the Manchester Institution in 1827. The subject of this dramatic portrait is the young black American Shakespearean actor, Ira Aldridge, who had just begun to play the role of Othello. This would later make him a household name throughout Europe. Aldridge died in 1867, having taken up British nationality. The artist was born in Plymouth, was a pupil of Reynolds, and painted this work in his eighties.

city states of Ancient Greece and their modern counterpart, Manchester.

Work on the building began in 1829 on the corner of Mosley Street and Princess Street, initially one of Manchester's most fashionable residential districts but which was then beginning to take on the commercial identity that characterises it today. The building was completed in 1835 and, in the meantime, negotiations to persuade George IV to grant his royal patronage to the Manchester Institution were successfully brought to a conclusion and the prefix 'royal' was added to its name. In 1827, even before the building was properly finished, the Royal Manchester Institution purchased from its first exhibition James Northcote's portrait of the celebrated black actor Ira Aldridge in his role as *Othello, the Moor of Venice*, painted in the previous year.

From the start, the Royal Manchester Institution instigated many important enterprises, creating strong links between the worlds of art, education and commerce. In 1838, rooms in the basement became the first home to the School of Design, the forerunner of the present day Faculty of Art and Design at the Manchester Metropolitan University. It made sense to invest in home-grown creative talent rather than importing designs for fabrics from London and, to support this initiative, examples of the fine and decorative arts were acquired for the institution. This policy, still in place today, is largely responsible for the richness and variety of the collection.

The general public were encouraged to make use of the Gallery within the institution, although the 6d it cost in 1846 to gain admission was a substantial amount of money for a working man of the time. All manner of cultural events were organised by what was then still a private enterprise – exhibitions, concerts and lectures being foremost on the agenda. In 1858, a year after the celebrated Manchester Art Treasures exhibition, the great Victorian critic John Ruskin, supporter of Turner and the Pre-Raphaelites, delivered one of his most famous and influential lectures at the Gallery. In 1882 the Royal Manchester Institution's building and its collection were given over to the city and it became the Manchester Art Gallery. An agreed sum of £4000 was set aside to be spent annually on purchases over the next twenty years. The following decade saw a flurry of picture buying, and it became common knowledge that the Manchester committee was always prepared to buy the biggest picture available at the Royal Academy exhibitions. In 1889 the committee paid £4000 for the huge work, *Captive Andromache*, painted by the President of the Royal Academy, Lord Leighton. In doing so, they outbid the cities of Birmingham and Liverpool in order to secure for their city what was a highly visible and expensive cultural trophy.

Over the years the Gallery has benefited from many generous donations that have shaped the collection. Charles Rutherston's 1925 bequest was significant in this respect as were those of Thomas Greg, the Beatson Blair brothers, Dr David Lloyd Roberts and Mr and Mrs Edgar Assheton-Bennett. The initiatives of curators and directors have further enriched the collection; for example, in the 1930s Lawrence Haward, an inspired curator, set up a purchasing scheme for the contemporary decorative arts, buying from department stores and manufacturers. More recently, curators have been actively acquiring contemporary art and design work. The role of the Corporate Patrons and The Friends, and other agencies such as the National Art Collections Fund and the Victoria and Albert Museum Purchase Grant Fund, have been crucial in enabling this to continue, as have the activities of the Contemporary Art Society's Special Collecting Scheme. The latter, funded by National Art Council Lottery grants, has enabled the Gallery to enhance its purchasing power for obtaining contemporary art and crafts. The Gallery is not simply a showcase for the permanent collection; it also runs an adventurous programme of temporary exhibitions and related educational activities designed to bring art in all its forms to as broad an audience as possible.

In the early 1890s, with remarkable foresight, the City Council purchased the land behind Manchester Art Gallery and then in 1938, after various schemes for building a new art gallery in Piccadilly Gardens had fallen through, the city purchased Charles Barry's impressive Athenaeum to act as an adjunct to the Gallery proper. Built in 1837–39, it is a virtuoso exercise in the Italian Palazzo style of the fifteenth and sixteenth centuries, and was so admired at the time that its distinctive features were echoed in many of the new warehouses that were springing up within the vicinity. The recent linking and refurbishing of these two great nineteenth-century buildings and the construction of new exhibition spaces has been the fulfilment of a long-standing need to allow greater public access to the works of the collection.

The building that now connects the Gallery and Athenaeum has been designed by Michael Hopkins & Partners. It is a discreet and elegant piece of contemporary architecture which compliments and enhances the original buildings. The interior spaces of the original buildings have also been decorated in keeping with their function as a modern art gallery, and the clarity of expression and simple elegance of Barry's rooms have been deliberately echoed in the interiors of the modern building. The former theatre, added to the top floor of the Athenaeum after a fire in 1873, accommodates a new display of the decorative art collections designed by Casson Mann. The practical result of all this development has been to double the display area previously available to the Gallery.

Coming in from the street, the visitor walks past the Ionic columns of the main facade and goes through the great doorway directly into the imposing entrance hall. Closed off from the outside world, everything about this resonant space is designed to enhance its identity as a site of almost sacred significance. Around its upper register are the casts taken from the Parthenon sculptures that were brought to England in 1816. Donated by George IV in 1824, a number of them depict the battle of the Centaurs and Lapiths, symbolising the victory of the rational over the irrational and proclaiming the now discredited nineteenth-century belief in the universal relevancy of Greek culture as the hallmark of a civilised society.

On leaving the familiar spaces of the old Gallery, visitors move into the spectacular centrepiece of the remodelled building, a transparent equivalent in glass and steel of the stone-built atrium they have just left behind. Cutting diagonally through this space, the clean, exposed forms of the staircase act as a reminder of how closely contemporary functional design can relate to modern sculptural practice. As the neo-Greek building separates the visitor and the exhibits from the living world, so this space allows the inner and outer worlds to interact, securing, maintaining and making evident the links between the Gallery, its contents and the world around it. From the upper floor a spectacular panorama unfolds, revealing the splendour and variety of Manchester's architectural heritage. Views can be seen of Alfred Waterhouse's neo-Gothic Town Hall (1867–77) and the formidable bulk of its extension (1934–38), designed by E. Vincent Harris as a twentieth-century homage to the great cloth halls of thirteenth-century Flanders. Inside the rooms, carefully situated windows offer pixilated views of Chinatown and reveal unexpected glimpses of the incisively sculpted stonework details of the exterior walls of the Gallery. These visual links with the city symbolise the Gallery's identity as an integral part of the urban fabric, formed by and expressive of its cultural, political, social and geographical context.

However impressive the building may be, it is essentially a stage for our interaction with the works that it holds: a site designed to stimulate our visual sensibilities. The new galleries and their contents encourage an opening of the mind and an engagement of the senses. To walk into these spaces is to enter a web of an almost infinite number of interrelated connections that can be made and enjoyed. Within these walls we enter into a communion with the living and the dead; we encounter the traces that remain of those who have died and who, consciously or otherwise, have left these objects behind to bear witness to their existence.

**Untitled** 1986
Keith Piper (born 1960)
Emulsion on canvas, 218.4 x 213.4 cm

It takes a moment to register the presence of American military helicopters (from a photograph by Tim Page in 1965) moving across the impassive and imperious features of a 10th–13th-century Benin sculpture of a priest or king. The stark combining of these two images, presented in a striking contrast of black and orange, make this an unforgettable visual metaphor of the continuation of legitimised violence situated at the root of colonialist expansion, which was such a major element in the creation of the wealth of Europe and America in the 19th century. Piper has used methods of collage and juxtaposition, rather than traditional forms of narrative, which allow the viewer greater space to come to an understanding of what this powerful image may suggest.

What is the significance of these fragments of human activity, these objects, art works and artefacts that have been set apart from the normal run of human existence to rest in this privileged setting? They are physical embodiments of inherited understandings of the world, allegories made up of symbolic figures and events that communicate both the simple and complex facts of basic human experience. This process is not restricted to the creation of pictures and sculptures alone; our need to decorate and embellish objects of practical use seems to be a universal one. Such creative acts are realisations of the necessity to pass on significant stories to those for whom we hold the earth in trust. We can learn from such stories, even, perhaps, be healed by them. The Gallery may be understood as a collection of these stories – stories which may hold publicly intended meanings and purposes but which also embrace the private meanings given by individuals and other communities who now have access to the work.

**Charger** c.1670
Thomas Toft (died 1689)
Earthenware with slip-trailed decoration
Diameter 42.5 cm

This rare dish represents one of the highest achievements of the English pottery tradition. Thomas Toft was a designer and craftsman of consummate skill who lived and worked in Staffordshire during the late 17th century. His compositions are masterful. Working within the extreme limitations of a circular design, and using a very difficult medium, he has produced an economical and supremely decorative motif. The image is drawn by trailing watered-down clay, or slip, onto the surface of the plate. The plate shows a scene from the English Civil War in which the beleaguered King Charles II hid in an oak tree to escape Cromwell's troops. The king's head is just visible peeping out from amongst the oak leaves. Ownership of this extravagant and expensive commemorative plate would make one's political sympathies very evident. The plate is part of the important Greg Collection of English Pottery (numbering nearly 1,000 objects) that was given to the Gallery in 1904.

Is it possible that these objects can be read as responses to universal experiences, more or less shared by us all, regardless of race, class, creed or gender? Is it possible to believe that one age, or even one person, can communicate directly to another across the boundaries of time, place and circumstance? The capacity of humans to do terrible things to each other is not restricted to the past or to other 'less civilised' societies, but is being enacted at every moment, in different ways, everywhere in the world. It is not enough to assert that art's only function is to be beautiful. Art deals with what it is to be human. We cannot ignore the realities of poverty, fear, homelessness, exile, social or political injustice, and not least, our own mortality.

These are the spaces in which art, of whatever kind, operates. Art inevitably encompasses notions and realities of power, exclusion, luxury and its opposite – the shadows and substance of life itself.

Art works and artefacts inevitably lose some of their original meanings and significances. They have not always been housed in museums and many of the works in the Manchester Art Gallery were not initially construed as works of art. In today's society, it can no longer be assumed, as perhaps the Victorians could, that there is a common currency of knowledge that can be triggered by classical myths, the Christian story or the belief systems that underpinned the British Empire. In their voyage to Manchester from the tombs of ancient Egypt, the devotional and liturgical setting of Renaissance churches or the opulent homes of great Victorian merchants, the significance of the objects and their audience has changed. In turn, modern gallery visitors become the producers of new meanings, transforming the objects' significance for their own purposes.

In these gallery spaces we come across thousands of representations of human beings: real or imaginary, young or old, beautiful or ugly, the famous and infamous, the anonymous, mythical or prosaic. We see them set within their frames, alone or in company, naked or clothed, in all kinds of positions and conditions, in moments of happiness, exaltation or grief. As well as considering those depicted, consider also the invisible presences, the shadows that stand behind the depictions – those who commissioned the works, who made them, who owned and used them. And, not least, think about our own presence as we stand, like so many previous generations of visitors, before these mute but expressive works.

The static objects set within the Gallery demand our imaginative interaction to animate them, to give them a voice and make them our own. Art responds to and charts public *and* private histories. *The Crucifixion*, a work probably produced in Duccio's workshop in early fourteenth-century Siena (see page 85), is a case in point. For most of us, seen within its gallery setting, it is primarily a beautiful object connected to a major Western artist. For its original audience, its greatest significance was as a tool for the communication of the Christian faith. In our more secular age, many of us would respond more directly to an expression of personal experience, such as that represented in *Sir Thomas Aston at the Deathbed of his Wife* (1635), John Souch's public manifestation of his patron's grief at the death of his wife in childbirth (see page 86). In regarding this image, we are given the opportunity, to some extent, to partake of Sir Thomas Aston's grief and to consider our own mortality. It is a powerful example of art's ability to make present what is in fact invisible or absent. The Tang funeral piece of a horse and rider (c. AD 706), so beautiful and apparently self-contained, was within its own culture an elegant marker of death (see page 83). However, to second, third and fourth generation descendants of Chinese ancestry it may signal (however distantly) the culture of which they were once an integral part. Looking out from the Gallery at the bustling street life of Manchester's Chinatown and the surrounding area, the links between the Gallery's objects and our own existence become obvious.

Lord Leighton's *Captive Andromache* (c.1888), painted at the height of the Empire, originated from a passage in Homer's epic poem, the *Iliad*, which is concerned with the siege of the city of Troy, its destruction and the aftermath (see page 56). The theme of the painting – the reality of exile as experienced by its central, black-draped figure – is as pertinent today as it has been at any time in history. It is a measure of the artist's peculiar talent that such a tragic narrative is conveyed by such a sumptuous piece of decoration.

A painting's purpose can be deliberately unostentatious – to remind the viewer to pay attention to the ordinariness of things and to the painter's skill in capturing the look, texture, space, place and time of such things. The meticulously rendered *Still Life: Fruit, Goblet and Salver* (c.1660) by Willem Kalf, for example, presents a moment frozen into immobility (see page 24). Using the same medium of oil paint in a completely different way, David Cox in *Rhyl Sands* (c.1855), with hardly any apparent effort or show of detail, evokes the immediacy of experience in presenting the effects of a sudden gust of wind as it blew across Rhyl sands on a particular moment in the high summer of that year (see page 45). Such things are precious and a joy for ever.

There is also, of course, painting for delight and pure visual pleasure: in Gainsborough's painting, *Peasant Girl in a Wood Gathering Faggots* (1782), one can almost taste the fluidity, transparency, colour and vibrancy coming off the picture's surface (see page 64). However, the work is also an example of the transformational powers of painting; through Gainsborough's art, the reality of

***Hylas and the Nymphs*** 1896
John W. Waterhouse (1849–1917)
Oil on canvas, 98.2 x 163.3 cm

Highly popular in its own time, Waterhouse's painting of the seduction and murder of an innocent youth by a group of wistful looking water nymphs became popular once again in the 1970s, and is now one of the most well-known images in British art. Innocence, temptation, desire, sexuality, malice and murder all meet together in this very English rendering of the Greek myth of Hylas, one of the Argonauts on Jason's expedition to capture the Golden Fleece. He was the handsome young companion of Hercules who, when sent to fetch water on the island of Mysia, never returned but was dragged to his death by these sweet-faced teenage *femmes fatales*. A quintessential image of the Victorian period, it still holds its power to attract and trouble today.

**Water Jug** 1995
Designed by Shannon O'Neill (born 1971)
Made by Shannon O'Neill with Naylor
Brothers, London
Silver. Height 35 cm

A virtuoso piece, made by Shannon O'Neill
whilst still a student in three-dimensional
design at the Manchester Metropolitan
University. The students were asked to
design a water jug suitable for a company
boardroom. This elegantly shaped silver jug
has an outward curving belly beneath a deep
inset lip and the upper body tapers back
towards a high sweeping handle. The sides
are decorated with evenly chased vertical
lines simulating rivulets of water. The silver
exterior contrasts with its gilt interior.
Shannon O'Neill won the Young Designer
Silversmith of the Year Award in 1995.

rural poverty has been made into something beautiful, even appealing. The
ambiguous manner in which this object at once addresses and avoids the issues
central to its subject only makes the painting even more telling. It is little wonder
that Gainsborough has been called the Mozart of painting.

In a speech made in 1930 Lawrence Haward declared, 'Art museums which at one
end of the scale include the rarest and most precious treasures devised for man's
pleasure should not neglect the simplest and most humble objects of everyday
use.' Manchester Art Gallery's holdings in the decorative arts are one of its
distinctive strengths. Designed objects, however decorated or embellished, give us
something of the real world itself rather then the representations of the world
provided by paintings and sculpture. Such objects are made from the stuff that is
all around us, raw materials that are mined, gathered, harvested and put through
various technical processes to result in the works set before us. The ceramic pot
was once earth or clay, made malleable through water, modelled, moulded,
incised, glazed and then fired in a kiln, going through a complex chemical process
to result in the object that is found in the gallery cabinet, now relatively secure
from the accidents of time and circumstance.

Such objects are evidence of the need, invention and ingenuity of humankind.
They show the turn of the hand, the touch of the fingers, the blow of the chisel or
the caress of the paint brush. A pot may bear the traces of its making and its
passage through history, time and space – each chip and crack, each loss and
repair the result of it being part of the world and, as such, it has an affirmative
quality that should be valued.

Occasionally, however, the form of an artefact can be so immaculate as to suggest
that its existence came into being fully fledged, without the intervention of any
human agency. Shannon O'Neill's *Water Jug* (1995) for example, is a celebration
and elevation of the ordinary but essential element of water. It is a vessel made to
contain and pour water: a simple, fundamental activity which is granted, through
the beauty of this object, an almost sacramental status. Until held, the jug seems
as apparently fluid and 'formless', as absent of colour and as reflective as water
itself. Like a piece of *haute couture* or a Formula One racing car, the piece is an
exemplar of excellence which acts as a catalyst to other designers. However, for
every piece produced through such skill, there are other, more robust objects
which form the stuff of the everyday, often manufactured in their hundreds or
thousands. Such objects can be bizarre and extraordinary, like the *Marshmallow
Love Seat* (1956) made by Herman Miller and designed by George Nelson
Associates, which characterises an entire epoch and suggests a creative approach
that hinges on the simple thrill of creating something new, distinctive and fun.

The works collected in these galleries reinvigorate our visual sensibilities. Looking
at them in surroundings that are set apart from everyday life allows us to ponder
on our relationship with these objects and to enjoy the pleasure of imagining and

*Marshmallow Love Seat* 1956
Designed by George Nelson Associates
Manufactured by Herman Miller, 1956–63
Aluminium and steel, upholstered in vinyl.
Height 130.5 cm

A piece of sculpture or functional object?
This distinctive and somewhat oddly titled
piece of furniture epitomises an innovative
era of American interior design, which was
characterised by an adventurous and wide-
ranging reconsideration of the relationships
between furniture, its look, its function and
its setting. Only a few hundred of these
'Love Seats' were produced. Despite its
romantic and organic title, the round
individual cushions and the sparse linear
and visible skeletal form of the supporting
structure reveal the period's fascination with
things scientific. Customers could choose
fabric, vinyl or naugahyde upholstery, and
also which colour combinations they
preferred: orange, pink and purple was the
most popular combination.

*Above, and detailed overleaf:*
**Ginger Jar** 1911
Designed by Richard Joyce (1871–1931)
Manufactured by Pilkington's Tile and
Pottery Company
Earthenware, metal lustres. Height 26.7 cm

Joyce was a prolific and accomplished artist,
specialising in beautifully realised designs of
animals and fish.

entering different worlds. The root principle of human creation is the imagination, what the nineteenth-century French poet and critic, Charles Baudelaire,
called, 'the Queen of the Faculties'. Free imaginative play is a significant action, an
end in itself as well as a powerful source of creativity and problem-solving.

To allow this to happen certain barriers may need to be broken down as the
American thinker, Susan Sontag, has suggested: 'What is more important now, is
to recover our senses. We must learn to see more, to hear more, to feel more … the
aim of all commentary on art should be to make works of art and by analogy our
own experience more, rather than less, real to us.' The sentiment is echoed in
D.H. Lawrence's realisation that, 'Ours is an excessively conscious age. We *know*
so much, we feel so little.'

When we open ourselves up to the gift of art, extraordinary things can happen.
In 1959, the art critic Edwin Mullins stood on the steps of Manchester Art Gallery,
having just visited an exhibition of paintings by L.S. Lowry. 'After spending an
hour with his pictures', he wrote, 'one descends the steps into Mosley Street into
a world that still belongs to Lowry. Having compelled one to tune into his wavelength, the wavelength persists … slowly the world of reality returns, but it has
been insensibly transfigured by the experience. One has borrowed his eyes for a
while, and then handed them back, but the memory remains'.

upclose

The image of a mother with her infant child is a perennial theme of Western art, and was one of Henry Moore's life-long concerns. This relatively small sculpture is an important early work, begun soon after his return from a scholarship in Italy where he was greatly impressed by the work of Masaccio and Michelangelo. It is sculpted from the soft, easily workable limestone that is found around the borders of Oxfordshire and Warwickshire.

Avant-garde artists working at this time were fascinated by the diversity and richness of world cultures, appropriating motifs and styles in the hope of giving their art a universal significance and resonance. This sculpture reveals Moore's affinity for the great block-like forms of Mayan pre-Columbian sculpture. Equally discernible are echoes of African art and the work of Picasso, Braque, Modigliani and especially the English sculptors, Epstein and Dobson.

The resulting work reveals the artist's deep love and understanding of natural forms. Making a timeless and universal statement, it celebrates the fierce pride of motherhood, and the conflicting imperative for a mother to protect her child as well as teach it independence.

*Mother and Child* 1925
Henry Moore (1898–1986)
Hornton stone, height: 56 cm

The Latin inscription beneath the image, which translates as 'Mary Full of Grace', makes it clear that this has been painted in honour of the Virgin Mary. Her child's sculptural form suggests his divine status, while the bird is a sign of his pre-ordained sacrifice. As one hand is planted firmly against his mother's face, the other is raised, fingers outstretched, reaching for, if not quite touching, her hand upon which the goldfinch or *cardellino* has come to rest. According to popular belief, as Christ made his way to his place of execution 33 years later, such a bird flew low over his head. As it drew a thorn from the crown around his forehead, a drop of Christ's blood stained its breast and has remained there ever since as a mark of the bird's compassion.

Graceful lines, glorious colour and elegant refinement mingle with a sculptural strength to reveal that this anonymous Florentine painter, working in the manner of Bernardo Daddi, has well assimilated the combined influences of the Sienese and Florentine traditions of painting.

This painting would probably have been part of a larger sequence of images that would have made up an impressive altarpiece. Now it stands alone as an exquisite object that has survived the vicissitudes of time, declaring the universal nature of the love between a mother and her child and the ability of humankind to create objects of great beauty that transcend the historical circumstances of their making.

***Virgin and Child and Goldfinch***
Follower of Bernardo Daddi (c.1290–1348)
Egg tempera on panel with gold ground,
62 x 32.2 cm
Purchased with the assistance of the V&A Purchase Grant Fund

The artist's best known work, this painting represents a rather glamourised vision of his own house on Skiddaw looking out over Derwent Water, with Scafell in the distance. Like an Agatha Christie novel or a Noël Coward play, it positively oozes period charm and overflows with nostalgia and sentiment. Little wonder then that although it has been seldom exhibited it is, in terms of sales of reproductions, the Gallery's most popular work. It is a piece of visual seduction which allows the viewer to partake, unobserved, of the untroubled daily round of these beautiful people as they bathe in the dazzling midsummer light of a Cumbrian afternoon, enjoying high tea, polite conversation and the company of a cat that appears to be unimpressed by their attempts to engage its interest. *Summer in Cumberland* is a perfect example of the kind of painting that was so popular in its day, before the onset of the Depression and the outbreak of the Second World War. Its very distance from the realities experienced by most of us today only serves to add to its discreet charm.

*Summer in Cumberland* 1925
James Durden (1878–1964)
Oil on canvas, 101.5 x 101.5 cm

An example of the modern grotesque, this piece playfully mingles the whimsical and threatening. Within its simple shape lurk mysterious, almost surreal animals and personages. Set against alternating bands of orange and blue, they engage in a sequence of enigmatic activities. Amongst them there is a man with a top hat and a straight beak who appears to be tossing two envelopes in the air, whilst another figure, his face animated with a maniacal grin, approaches, a leafing cane in his hand.

This elegant and fantastical piece was designed by Bertil Vallien, one of the leading designers and makers of contemporary glassware. He and his wife run the Afors Glassworks, part of the Kosta Boda firm which was originally founded in 1742 to supply glass for the Swedish royal palaces. Today they work with a small team of artists, designers and craftsmen to produce unique pieces using techniques which, like those of the potter, have changed little since Egyptian times. This glass bowl is distinctly northern European in concept, and is the result of a complex series of operations – from its initial design to its formation in the glassworks. The introduction of colour, the engraving of the design and the sandblasting all work together to give this piece its unique character.

**Bowl** 1987
Bertil Vallien (born 1938)
Manufactured by Kosta Boda
Coloured glass, sandblasted
Height 23.5 cm

*Au Chat Botté* 1932
Ben Nicholson (1894–1982)
Oil on canvas, 92.3 x 122 cm

O n a short summer trip to Dieppe in 1932, Ben Nicholson came across a shop called Au Chat Botté or, in English, 'Puss in Boots'. On his return to London he completed this supremely elegant painting. Nine years later the artist recalled how he felt it was impossible in the painting to tell what was real and what was unreal, what was reflected and what was not. This, he wrote, '… created some kind of space or an imaginative world in which one could live'.

The basic ingredients of this picture owe everything to the example of the Cubist paintings of Picasso and Braque, but the result is the artist's own. It is a playful and elusive evocation of time, space, experience, memory and the processes of representation. The head of the sculptor Barbara Hepworth, who was to become Nicholson's wife in 1934, is reflected upon the glass frontage but seems to float mysteriously amongst the objects that lie beyond its transparent surface. The letters 'DIEPPE' stencilled upon the shop's window mischievously slide behind the contours of the painted jug that is placed so decisively within the space of the display area. Incisive drawing and flat, sensitively modulated veils of ambiguously muted colours weave together to make this one of the most lyrical and unforgettable 20th-century British paintings. Its fairy tale title is completely right for this playful exploration of illusion, deception and delight.

K alf was celebrated in his lifetime and for many years after as a master of illusionist painting. This still life celebrates the artifice of painting, its possibilities and limits. It reveals how mere pigment, artfully manipulated, can reproduce the fresh colour of the lemon; the spiralling twist of peel which reveals the succulent fruit within; the form and transparency of the two wine glasses, and the absorption and reflection of light as it falls upon the different objects set before the painter's gaze. This canvas declares the painter's ability to evoke with consummate skill the pleasures of sight, taste, touch and ownership. Traces of the process by which this illusion has been created have been completely effaced; no visible brush marks, impasto or pentimenti disturb its immaculate surface.

In 1797 the great poet and philosopher, Goethe, wrote of one of the artist's earlier works, 'One must see this picture in order to understand in what sense art is superior to nature and what the spirit of man imparts to objects when it views them with creative eyes. There is no question, at least for me, if I had to choose between the golden vessels or the picture, that I would choose the picture'.

The composition of this canvas, its colour, texture and the balancing of light and shade, work together to create an image of apparent inviolability, suggesting that these painted objects will, unlike the objects they depict, escape the ravening clutches of time.

In the 19th century works such as this became touchstones of excellence, as artists like Manet and Cézanne used the genre to explore and extend the possibilities of representation.

*Still Life: Fruit, Goblet and Salver*
c.1660
Willem Kalf (1619–93)
Oil on canvas, 58.0 x 50.7 cm
Bequest of Mr and Mrs Edgar Assheton-Bennett

This giant vase in the form of a pineapple was commissioned by Manchester Art Gallery for the Gallery café in 1994. It was the largest work that Malone had created up to that point in her career, and it represented an enormous technical challenge. The finished vase stands over a metre high. It took nine months to complete and weighs over 130 kilos. Its sculptural power is immediately apparent, and *Queen Pineapple* is a perfect example of how contemporary ceramicists are challenging the once rigid boundaries that divided the work of the artist from that of the craftsperson. The vase is completely made by hand, and each element has been individually crafted. The vase was developed using one of the oldest methods of pot-making – the rolling of clay into coils which are then laid in a spiral formation to create the basic pot shape. Then, piece by piece, each hand-modelled, diamond-shaped segment was added to its exterior. Its surface is decorated with crystalline glazes, which develop as the pot is being fired, creating a distinctive and unique translucent sheen.

Kate Malone has called the pineapple her 'dream fruit' and the fruit's extraordinary structure, its geometrical precision, natural beauty and wild exoticism are qualities found in much of her other work, particularly her ceramics inspired by the underwater life of the sea. Surprisingly, the pineapple has a long and honoured history as a design subject. The fruit was introduced into Europe by Christopher Columbus in 1493 and for many centuries it was synonymous with luxury, sensory extravagance and hospitality. Throughout the 1700s and 1800s, it was *the* symbol for table-top decorations and its image has been used in all manner of situations, for example, on the gate posts and lintels of country houses. The motif was a particular favourite of Staffordshire potters in the 18th century who evidently enjoyed using the fruit in a variety of ways, especially in the form of yellow-glazed teapots.

*Queen Pineapple* 1994–95
Kate Malone (born 1959)
Hand-built stoneware with crystalline glazes. Height 970 cm
Commissioned with assistance from The Friends of Manchester City Galleries

Lucien Freud has written that a '... moment of complete happiness never occurs in the creation of a work of art. The promise of it is felt in the act of creation but disappears towards the end completion of the work. For it is then that the painter realises that it is only a picture he is painting.'

One can imagine this young woman sitting passively before the painter's intense scrutiny as her likeness, stroke by immaculately calculated stroke, coalesced into the image we now in turn scrutinise. Her lustrous eyes look out as we look in; she gazes at something over our shoulders, her damp, slightly compressed lips suggesting the hint of a smile or the possibility of speech. In reality the sitter and the painter of this picture are absent and yet, through this image, they are both in some mysterious way before us. This compelling painting reveals both the power and limitation of art in trying to represent the real, and its endless ability to fascinate, attract and disturb.

The work has been created with the scrupulous attention and tact of a Flemish painter of the 15th century. Its essentially symmetrical balance is broken by the side parting of the young woman's hair and the unexpected presence of the ear, adorned with a simple, understated earring. It charts, with a vaguely disturbing exactitude, the precise way in which the cool studio light effects an infinite series of tonal and colourful modulations on flesh, conveying its translucency and the way skin receives, absorbs and reflects the light. We can track the smoothness of her skin as it stretches across her forehead, defines her nose and moves around the contours of her face. Yet for all this accumulation of the visual detail of the exterior surface of her face and modest costume, what do we actually learn about this person?

*Girl with a Beret* 1951
Lucien Freud (born 1921)
Oil on canvas, 35.5 x 25.6 cm

*Mary Cornwallis* c.1580–85
George Gower (c.1540–96)
Oil on panel, 117 x 94 cm

flat, mask-like portrayal of the features. As the artist's friend, the miniaturist Thomas Hilliard, said to Queen Elizabeth I, portraits look, 'best in plain lynes without shadowing'.
In this superbly ordered composition, however, the sitter's appraising gaze gives some suggestion of a determined personality. The painting illustrates to perfection the concluding lines of one of Shakespeare's most celebrated sonnets:

*So long as men can read and eyes can see*
*So long lives this, and this gives life to thee.*

The subject is portrayed frontally so that the sumptuousness of her dress, silk ruff, jewellery and fashion accessories may be fully appreciated. Her linen sleeves, decorated with blackwork embroidery, are visible through the semi-transparent over-sleeves of silk or lawn and her skirt is embellished with embroidered strap-work, the whole ensemble revealing the period fashion for mingling floral motifs with geometric designs.

Her plain black velvet gown is set off by five ropes of pearls which also feature in her headdress and girdle, from which hangs a white silk ribbon and a jewelled cameo or miniature of a bearded man. Her fan bears the arms of the Cornwallis family of Brome in Suffolk. Mary Cornwallis was secretly married to William Bourchier, Earl of Bath, but his family disapproved and their marriage was annulled.

George Gower was born into a Yorkshire family as a gentleman and, in 1581, he was appointed Serjeant Painter to Queen Elizabeth I. Along with Hilliard, he was one of the most sought after artists of his time.

Against the prevailing trend amongst European artists, English portraitists of the Tudor period preferred to create heraldic, iconic images which revealed, not so much the sitter's psychological character, as their status and wealth. Accordingly, dramatic lighting and facial idiosyncrasies were eschewed in favour of a

This unique panel of 35 earthenware tiles, depicting a young Persian falconer in a landscape setting, is painted in underglaze, metal oxides and colour slips. The director of the manufacturers at the time was William Burton, who helped to develop Pilkington's as a company that could produce wares to match the great pottery of the past, particularly that of Ancient Greece and, as in this example, the Islamic countries of the medieval period. He encouraged a small group of designers, including George Mitchell Forsyth who became art director at the firm, to produce a wide variety of designs of great style and quality. This panel shows the eclectic nature of English 19th-century and early 20th-century design and a love of things exotic. The influence of Persian design seen at work here also influenced the stage and costume designers for the *Ballet Russes*, the painter Matisse and the dress designer Paul Poiret, and became a fundamental ingredient of Art Deco.

*The Persian Falconer* c.1910
Attributed to Gordon Mitchell Forsyth (1879–1952)
Manufactured by Pilkington's Tile and
Pottery Company
Earthenware, painted under glaze
Height 109.2 cm
Gift of Pilkington's Tiles Ltd

The cheetah so elegantly displayed in this painting was a gift from the Governor of Madras to George III. The painting commemorates an event organised at Windsor Castle in July 1764 which was designed to demonstrate the animal's prowess as a killer. Its two Indian handlers stand by, ready to release the animal so that it can kill the stag that had been tethered nearby.

George Stubbs is best known for his paintings of horses but he painted a number of other animals, including many exotic ones such as this. Despite the almost ludicrous and truly barbaric nature of this event, the animal and its handlers have lost nothing of their dignity in the painting. The oddly stilted poses and soft, atmospheric handling of this beautifully organised image give the composition a curious, dream-like quality. This is not just a trophy piece, for under the surface there is an aura of unease and anticipation that compromises the almost classical equilibrium of this precisely observed event. Stubbs has shown us not the kill or the attack, so frequently the subject of hunting scenes painted by himself and his contemporaries, but the moment just before. The alert beast was apparently terrified, but stands ready for action, its tawny fur bristled, the brilliant red cap yet to be unfurled and the leash around its back yet to be released.

The stage-managed killing did not quite go to plan. The stag repelled the cheetah and, by way of a reward, was presented with a commemorative silver collar and its freedom.

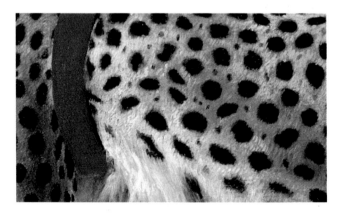

*Cheetah and Stag and Two Indians* 1765
George Stubbs (1724–1806)
Oil on canvas, 180.7 x 273.3 cm
Purchased with the assistance of the National Art
Collections Fund (Eugene Cremetti Fund)

The setting is the Circus Maximus in Ancient Rome and the event is the chariot race that marks the culmination of Wallace Irving's great novel *Ben Hur*, published in 1880. To suggest the release of elemental energy that drives the competing teams forward, the artist has depicted the horses with all four legs raised off the ground. The spectacular depiction of the amphitheatre, the dramatic postures of the riders and the agitated gestures of the crowd pale into insignificance as we gaze at the arched necks and flared nostrils of the horses hurtling towards the finishing post, heedless of our presence before them.

Conceived in a completely different spirit to Manet's innovative images of horse races painted in the 1860s and early 1870s, this highly detailed painting displays a virtuoso handling of perspective which creates an irresolvable tension between the flatness of the canvas and the illusion it conveys. As with a Hollywood spectacular, we gladly accept the conventions of the genre and willingly suspend our disbelief in order to enjoy the frisson that is the purpose of the whole painting: the thrill of it all.

Von Wagner was a Hungarian painter who specialised in panoramic spectacles featuring detailed archaeological reconstructions. This canvas, like the novel that inspired it, is one of the many 19th- and 20th-century works that present the distant past as a time when people were driven by the same emotions, ambitions, hopes and fears that motivate us today.

***The Chariot Race*** 1898
Alexander von Wagner
(1838–1919)
Oil on canvas, 138.3 x 347 cm
Bequest of Mrs E. M. Higgins

This piece was designed by the Victorian architect and designer William Burges, for his own bedroom in his apartment at 15 Buckingham Street, The Strand, in London. He was famous for his originality, quirkiness and a highly eclectic approach to design. Burges' buildings, such as Cardiff Castle and his later home, The Tower House, Melbury Road, London, are characterised by a sense of fun and a desire to give pleasure.

About three years after he had created the chest of drawers, he added the stand in order to display his middle-eastern, Indian and Oriental artefacts and examples of Indian and Islamic textiles. The two pieces were separated after his death and have only recently been brought together.

The stand is made from gilded pine and is carved with Gothic columns and tracery, figures of birds and mice, and Islamic domes. It is set with small panels of mirrored glass and richly embroidered Indian velvet. The cabinet itself is gilded and decorated by the artist, Charles Rossiter, who painted humorous vignettes in reference to the contents of the drawers. For example,

the pictures include an old woman darning, a man with a towel, and a gentleman trying on a shirt. On one side of the cabinet there is an image of a gentleman in fresh flannels and the other side features a 'navvy' wearing dirty working clothes.

This piece is very different from the work of Burges' early years, represented in the Gallery's collection by his escritoire which was made in the mid-1860s and clearly reveals a kinship with the work of artists and designers of the Pre-Raphaelite movement. The piece is both bold and delicate, and its Gothic influence is worn lightly. Burges was probably also influenced by his friend, E.W. Godwin, whose interest in things Japanese can be discerned in the elegance of this extra-ordinary piece of furniture.

**Display cabinet on a chest of drawers**
1865–67 (chest of drawers); 1873 (stand)
William Burges (1827–81)
Chest painted by Charles Rossiter
Painted and gilded pine, decorated cut glass, textiles and marble. Height 233 cm
Purchase supported by The National Lottery through the Heritage Lottery Fund, with the assistance of the Corporate Patrons and The Friends of Manchester City Galleries

*The Storm* 1829–30
William Etty (1787–1849)
Oil on canvas, 91 x 104.5 cm

Exhibited at the Royal Academy in 1830, this allegorical painting was accompanied by an extract from Psalm 22 in its catalogue description: 'They cried unto thee, and were delivered: they trusted in thee, and were not confounded.' The painting is a visualisation of an idea: the need to put faith in the Lord even in the most extreme of circumstances.

The artist was born and died in York, although he lived most of his life in London, studied in Paris and visited Italy on several occasions. He was committed to the ideal of historical painting and studied the works of Titian, Tintoretto, Rubens and Van Dyck, as well as the painters associated with the Romantic movement, particularly Géricault and Delacroix whom the artist met in 1825. His work has the vigour, sexual energy and dark drama that animates the early work of Cézanne.

This painting was a favourite of the artist, and he regretted its sale to the Manchester Institution in 1832. Contrary to his normal practice, he wished to attain a 'harmony of colour by neutral tints' and not by the excessive use of colour for which he was well known and often criticised. It is, as one contemporary critic wrote, 'a picture of expression'. At once haunting and melodramatic, it manages to trouble our imagination. The pathetic frailty of their barque and the menacing, skull-like form of the billowing sail, isolated against the turbulent sea and sky, remind us of the power of painting to inspire private, hidden and unconscious meanings as well as the more evident, public ones.

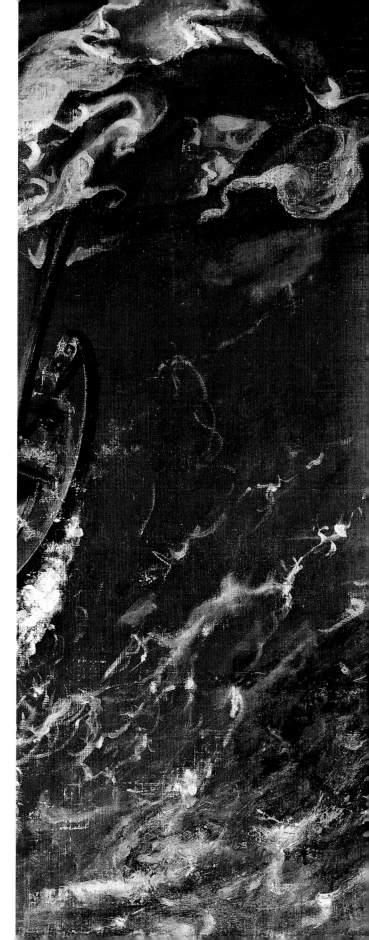

Turner made tours around Switzerland and Germany to produce saleable works for English collectors. His ambition was to create paintings that communicated the vividness of visual experience as immediately as possible, untrammelled by the conventional structures of pictorial tradition. The artist's late works especially irradiate light and are documents of intense subjectivity – the images of the world that he presents appear to be forever trembling on the verge of resolution and dissolution.

This view is of the German university city of Heidelberg, its famous castle set between the balancing forms of the bridge and church, visible high above the River Neckar. Working from sketches and drawings made on the spot, Turner first washed in simple bands of colour: cobalt blue, ultramarine and burnt sienna moving into yellow ochre on the right. Over this he has worked in more detail to further define the colour effects and the spatial dynamics – the reflections on the water and the solidity of the castle. Using opaque white paint and scratching out the top surface of pigment to reveal the white of the paper underneath, he has found a pictorial equivalent of the infinitely refracted modulations of the light, colour and space of the original scene.

One of 37 Turner watercolours in the collection, this was originally owned by James Thomas Blair who considered it to be the 'gem' of his collection. He donated it to Manchester Art Gallery on the stipulation that, as a watercolour and therefore sensitive to strong light, great care should be taken to preserve the vividness of its colours.

*Heidelberg: Sunset* c.1840–42
Joseph Mallord William Turner
(1775–1851)
Pencil, watercolour and bodycolour
with scraping out, 38 x 55.2 cm
Bequest of Mr James Thomas Blair

**The Bright Cloud** 1833–34
Samuel Palmer (1805–81)
Oil and tempera on mahogany panel,
23.3 x 32 cm
Purchased with the assistance of the V&A
Purchase Grant Fund and the National Art
Collections Fund

Palmer believed that nature was the sign and signature of a benevolent God and, accordingly, he ignored the historical realities of agrarian unrest all around him and presented the fertile valley of Shoreham in Kent as a terrestrial paradise.

Palmer's art owed much to his friendship with the visionary poet and artist, William Blake, his childhood reading of the Bible (especially the Psalms), and the poetry of Milton, whose epic verse *Paradise Lost* was probably the source of this composition:

> *... yon western cloud, that draws*
> *O'er the blue firmament a radiant white,*
> *And slow descends, with something*
> *heavenly frought.*

In 1828 Palmer, a gifted writer as well as an artist of unique sensibility, wrote of this valley with its 'mild reposing breadths of lawn and hill, shadowy glades and meadows, sprinkled and showered with a thousand pretty eyes, and buds, and spires, and blossoms gemm'd with dew ... clad in living green ... the motley clouding: the fine meshes, the aerial tissues, that dapple the skies of spring ...'

Palmer matched the intensity of this response to nature with a brilliant and complex technical process involving oil and tempera to create his richly textured compositions.

The aim of this painting is as simple as the means used to create it – it is a marvellous evocation of a windy day on a beach in North Wales. Cox was a popular and successful artist, a watercolourist, oil painter, teacher and author of manuals on drawing. He travelled throughout the picturesque regions of Britain and the Continent painting charming landscapes for a rapidly growing audience of middle-class collectors.

Cox loved to depict people in his works. Here we see a group of tourists fully absorbed in their recreational activities, and we can sense the artist's delight in translating their idiosyncratic movements into accents of colour. *Rhyl Sands* presents a vivid and immediate image. It may well have been painted in the open air but it is more likely that the painting was worked up in the studio from watercolour studies made on the spot. It is unusual not only in its lack of topographical detail (so typical of watercolours of the Victorian period and of much of the artist's other work), but also in its exquisite surface texture.

The assured handling of the thin scumbled paint and the harmonious succession of soft pinks, blues and greys suggests a relationship with the paintings of Boudin and Pissarro. In capturing how things feel, as much as how they are seen, this work becomes part of the revolution in painting that began with Turner and Constable and became a central tenet of the Impressionists.

*Rhyl Sands* c.1855
David Cox (1783–1859)
Oil on canvas, 45.8 x 63.5 cm
Bequest of Mr James Thomas Blair

This enamelled casket contains two tea caddies and a sugar box. Its delicate edges are protected by chased copper rococo mounts and the exterior of the objects contained inside are painted with images of idealised rustic scenes.

Enamels were first made on a commercial scale in England in the 1740s and were inspired by French jewelled and enamelled boxes. The copper was beaten on wooden forms to create the body of the piece that would then be enamelled. Enamel pieces varied in size and were very popular in the 18th century. They were used for a variety of purposes – snuffboxes, pillboxes or, as here, to hold tea. In this piece, green tea would be stored in one container and black tea in the other. The remaining caddy would have held either sugar or a mixed blend of teas.

The main area of production of enamel pieces was in South Staffordshire and the industry employed many French Huguenot craftsman who had come to England to escape religious persecution. This casket shows the skill of such workers – it was very difficult to produce enamels of this size with such a large number of colours. The decoration on the lid of this delicately formed piece is painted in the manner of Nicolaes Berchem who, until the end of the 19th century, was one of the most highly regarded Dutch 17th-century painters.

**Casket** c.1770 (shown open
and closed)
South Staffordshire, England
Enamel with chased gilt copper
mounts. Length 21 cm
Bequest of Harold Rabey

Laden, overburdened even, with allegorical significance, this is one of the many key images of the Victorian period belonging to the Gallery. A letter from the artist makes it evident that this obsessively detailed painting of a rustic swain and his sweetheart, flirting on a high summer's day in the Surrey landscape, can, amongst other things, be read as a visual diatribe against the Church of England's developing relations with Catholicism and its corresponding neglect of its pastoral duties.

The title, taken from a song in Shakespeare's *King Lear*, makes reference to Christ's charge to Saint Peter that he should be as a shepherd to his flock, the Church thereby assuming the role of a 'hireling shepherd'. In the painting, some of the sheep wander unseen into a neighbouring cornfield, others lie bloated on the grass and, on the lap of this village *femme fatale* (a latter-day Eve or, as her scarlet dress suggests, the Whore of Babylon as described in the *Book of Revelation*), a little lamb munches an unripe apple. As she is shown a Death's Head moth by her somewhat over-enthusiastic companion, she leans back, her hand coming to rest seductively close to his eager body.

Interesting as this use of the landscape as a means of conveying a religious message may be, it is the microscopic detailing, the complete lack of sympathy with the ability of the eye to see things more generally, that makes this painting so unforgettable. Everything is in clear focus and brilliant colour. Unsurprisingly, this painting was much admired by Salvador Dali.

*The Hireling Shepherd* 1851
William Holman Hunt (1827–1910)
Oil on canvas, 76.4 x 109.5 cm

Millais wrote that this painting was not intended to have a specific literary or biblical subject as had been the case with his earlier Pre-Raphaelite works. Instead it was intended 'to awaken by its solemnity the deepest religious reflection'.

It was painted at Annat Lodge in Perthshire, the Millais' family home, between autumn 1855 and early April the following year. The peak of Ben Vorlich can be seen in the distance. It is an elegiac painting, melancholy in mood and reminiscent of the poems of Tennyson that the artist was illustrating at the time, as well as a poem by Thomas Allingham called *Autumn Sonnet* that Millais admired. In the fading light four young girls, the eldest not yet 13, gather around a smouldering fire of fallen leaves. Sophie – the sister of Effie, the artist's wife – lets the russet-coloured leaves fall into the basket held by her sister Alice, whilst two village girls, chosen by Effie for their prettiness, look on, one gazing into the distance with an apple in her hand and the other leaning dreamily on her broom. It is a bitter-sweet meditation upon the cycle of life, the passage from innocence to experience and the inevitability of death and decay.

*Autumn Leaves* 1855–56
Sir John Millais (1829–98)
Oil on canvas, 104.3 x 74 cm

**Work** 1852–65
Ford Madox Brown (1821–93)
Oil on canvas, 137 x 197.3 cm

Conceived as a contemporary historical painting, *Work* illustrates a moral, social and political message. The biblical quotations on the frame, Brown's own catalogue entry and a sonnet he wrote on the painting all reinforce its didactic nature.

The background was painted entirely in the open air. The setting, Heath Street in Hampstead, is still recognisable today. The Victorians read their paintings, much as we might read a novel or view a film. The viewer is encouraged to scan the canvas, detail by glorious detail, and in doing so to construct for themselves the significance and meaning of the picture. Two men, the Christian socialist F.D. Maurice and the philosopher Thomas Carlyle, whose writing suggested the subject of this canvas, look out from under the shade of a tree at a group of 'navvies' hard at work in the sun.

The central figure, 'the British excavator', stands like a modern-day Greek god, whilst around him is a kaleidoscope of contemporary types, all of whom are related, positively or negatively, to the central theme of the painting. Rich and poor, male and female, old and young, urban and rural, employed and unemployed, industrious and idle – all are packed together in this crowded canvas. The key to the picture's purpose is the rich capitalist on horseback, his way barred by the workers below; the key to the heart of the painting is the young orphan girl, busy caring for her brothers and sisters.

During the revolutionary struggle in Russia in the early 1920s, the need to generate effective propaganda at every level was a national imperative. This chess set represents not only that struggle but also the growing distrust of avant-garde art to convey effectively the message of the Revolution. Chess was seen as a classless national pastime, as the slogans used at the All Union Congress made evident: 'Take Chess to the Workers!'

The white pieces represent the imperialist forces of repression. The Tsar is symbolised as a skeleton in tarnished armour, his lascivious queen leaning on a cornucopia of gold coins, whilst the pawns are modelled as enslaved serfs in chains. The opposing force is led by a factory worker and a peasant girl who holds in her right arm a bouquet of flowers.

*The Reds and the Whites*, designed in 1922
Designed by Natal'ya Yakolevno Dan'ko
(1892–1942)
Manufactured by the State Porcelain Factory,
Leningrad in 1936
Hard-paste porcelain, painted in overglaze
and gilt. Height varies from 5.5 to 11 cm
Purchased with the assistance of The Friends of the Manchester City Galleries and the MGC / V&A Purchase Grant Fund

Flanking them, two dashing Red Army guards watch over the opposing force's pawns, who are modelled as liberated peasants carrying sickles and sheaves of corn to represent the collective effort of industry and agriculture. This set is just one of many examples of art and design objects that were created in support of the Revolution.

Natal'ya Yakolevno Dan'ko trained as a sculptor and her work was often painted by her sister E. Dan'ko. The chess sets were exhibited in the shop window at the State Porcelain Factory in Leningrad. However, as they were comparatively expensive it is unlikely that they were bought in any quantity. Ironically, they became luxury items purchased by European collectors.

**Captive Andromache** c.1888
Lord Leighton (1830–96)
Oil on canvas, 197 x 407 cm
Purchased, following a public appeal, in 1889

B orn a doctor's son in Scarborough, Frederic Leighton received his artistic training on the Continent. Perhaps the most esteemed artist of his time, he was described by one commentator as a 'mixture of the Olympian Jove and a head waiter, a superb decorator and a superb piece of decoration'. Like many Victorian artists, despite being successful in his own time his work was subsequently derided. Now it may be seen in a more considered light: portentous, pretentious, self-important, coldly calculating, but nevertheless irresistible.

Leighton chose his subject carefully, interpreting a brief but significant passage in Homer's *Iliad* from which to develop this emotional, evocative and decorative piece. Hector refuses his wife Andromache's pleas not to return to the field of battle and prophesies the destruction of himself, his house and family. He foresees his widow in

exile: 'I see you there in Argos, toiling for some other woman at the loom and carrying water from an alien well, a hopeless drudge, with no will of your own.' This prediction comes true and Leighton uses this episode to create a svelte, mannered painting of immaculate surfaces and chromatic splendour.

Andromache is shown gazing intently at a happy family who are oblivious of her presence. She is at once central and marginalized. She may be the fulcrum of the composition but, in terms of the picture's narrative, she is the outsider, separated from the processional figures that flank her solitary form. Set against the receding perspective of buildings and the looming mass of the heavy, cloud-laden sky, she stands isolated, dark-robed and grief-stricken – a tragic heroine lost amongst a riot of opulent colours.

This painting's frame was designed by the artist, and bears the last six lines of a sonnet of his, beginning with:

*Mystery: lo! betwixt the Sun and Moon*
*Astarte of the Syrians: Venus Queen*
*Ere Aphrodite ever was.*

Christina Rossetti, the artist's sister, wrote in a poem dated 1856 that in her brother's work: 'One face looks out from all his canvases ... not as she is, but as she fills his dream.' Whoever was the subject of his canvases, Rossetti's paintings were ultimately the externalisation of his own fantasies and desires. He never completed his training as a painter and always felt dissatisfied with his art. In his own mind he was first and foremost a poet and was concerned only with his own private obsessions. A founder member of the Pre-Raphaelite Brotherhood, he took his inspiration from the writings of Dante, Mallory and Shakespeare. From the 1860s he began to paint pictures of voluptuous female figures, often from mythology, which have become icons of their age, redolent of an ambiguous and dangerous sexuality.

Rossetti's model for the main figure in this painting was Jane Morris, the wife of his close friend William Morris. She became his muse, his absorption and his lover. L.S. Lowry considered this to be 'the greatest picture in the world' and he was held captive by the work's compelling power. The paint may be thick and unwieldy, the colour crude and strong, the drawing distorted and bizarre, but the undeniable presence of this figure – cramped in her golden frame with a staring, sensual face – make this a powerful and disturbing image of male desire, fear and anxiety.

*Astarte Syriaca* 1875–77
Dante Gabriel Rossetti (1828–82)
Oil on canvas, 182.9 x 106.7 cm

Hunt, a committed Christian, believed in making his paintings as true as possible to the world that God had created, and went to extraordinary lengths to achieve this. *The Light of the World* was painted in moonlight, using a hut specially built in an orchard. The door was based on one in a dilapidated railway station building. The soulful face of Christ caused the artist a lot of trouble and was only finished after using several models, including Lizzie Siddal and Christina Rossetti. The lantern was made to Hunt's careful specification to incorporate his ideas of Christian symbolism. It has seven sides and seven circular openings, while the design of the apertures relate to paganism, the Jewish faith and Christianity. The lantern was acquired by the Gallery in 2001 and is now displayed adjacent to the painting, adding to our understanding of the artist's unique working method.

The first version of this image of Christ, travelling through the night to knock on the door of the human soul, was exhibited at the Royal Academy in 1854 with the text, 'Behold, I stand at the door, and knock: if any man hear my voice, and open the door, I will come into him, and will sup with him and he with me' (*Book of Revelation*, 3: 20). This second version was painted shortly after. Hunt also produced a third much later version. All three undertook extensive tours abroad, and the painting appeared in numerous engravings. It became one of the best known and enduring religious images of the 19th century. Van Gogh, for instance, regarded it as the symbol *par excellence* of the power of Christ.

*The Light of the World* 1851–60
William Holman Hunt (1827–1910)
Oil on canvas, 49.8 x 26.1 cm

*Sappho* 1877
Charles Mengin (1853–1933)
Oil on canvas, 230.7 x 151.5 cm
Gift of Thomas Lloyd

One of the top-selling postcards in the Gallery, this sombre painting is a visualisation of Sappho's evocative lines, 'I become paler than grass and in my distraction I seem to fail almost to the point of death'.

Born in the Greek island of Lesbos around 600 BC, Sappho was renowned as one of the greatest lyrical poets of her time. Plato called her the 'tenth muse'. Her work was largely destroyed over the years and now exists only in fragmentary form, but is still admired for its poetic power and emotional force. In the last 200 years or so, she has become an exemplar of female creativity, especially in the way that she gave voice to women's experiences. In the absence of precise information, legends and stories have been woven around her life, the most famous of which is the story of her suicide. Supposedly driven to it by unrequited love, she is said to have leapt to her death from the precipice at Leucadia. The character of Sappho has been reinvented many times, each epoch creating an image of the poet to suit its own needs. Today she has become a lesbian icon, a notion largely developed in the 19th century.

A pupil of Cabanel, Charles Mengin worked in the accepted academic manner of the time. He was a sculptor as well as a painter and exhibited regularly at the Paris Salon from 1876–1927. This painting was exhibited at the Paris Salon in 1877, the same year as the third Impressionist exhibition.

In the words of the artist, 'I do not want to avoid telling a story, but I want very, very much ... to give the sensation without the boredom of its conveyance. And the moment the story enters, the boredom comes upon you.' This painting is a visual and visceral shock. Bacon can portray like no one else the 'meatiness' of the human body and, in doing so, breaks down the carefully held distinction between ourselves and the animal kingdom.

The sprawling figure is developed from a specially commissioned photograph of his friend, Henrietta Moraes, taken by John Deakin. Half-seated, half-lying naked on a bed, she is a parody or pastiche of the countless 'seductive' nudes that inhabit the world of High Art. This is one of three similar compositions that survive and, although he knew the model well, Bacon preferred to work from photographs which allowed him to paint, not a superficial response to life, but its 'elemental state'.

Like a figure taken down from a crucifix or abandoned half-way through an autopsy, she confronts us from her reclining position on an extraordinary folding bed or sofa that threatens, coffin-like, to swallow her up. A pervading sense of unease permeates the canvas and nothing of the outside world intrudes upon the scene; the door is closed, she is locked away from the world. It is a compelling and dark vision of reality, what Bacon called 'the brutality of fact' – to him a permanent feature of human life that he found exemplified in literary works ranging from Aeschylus to T.S. Eliot.

*Portrait of Henrietta Moraes* 1965
Francis Bacon (1910–86)
Oil on canvas, 198 x 147 cm
Purchased with the assistance of the
Wilfred R. Wood Bequest and the MGC / V&A
Purchase Grant Fund

Peter Crutch was a fellow student of the artist at the Royal College of Art, a great dancer and stylish dresser. Hockney developed a hopeless crush on his heterosexual friend and this early painting is a quirky, pictorial confession of his affection, in effect a painted valentine. The artist made use of various stratagems to disguise, but not to hide, the nature of his feelings. The stencilled writing is intended to be read as 'who is the m[ost beautiful boy in the world]'. The graffiti-like writing and scrawled surfaces suggest the raw desperation of his feelings and are a strategy borrowed from artists who, at the time, were using such techniques to heighten the emotional and expressive power of their work.

In typical fashion, Hockney extended the portrait over two canvases in order to accommodate Peter's legs which were, he said, simply too beautiful to be left out. For all its apparent humour this is a confessional portrait, telling us as much, if not more, about the artist than the sitter it purports to represent. The artist's impossible desires are achieved by proxy in the capturing of his would-be lover's features on the canvas. Later, Hockney produced a series of prints inspired by the poems of the Alexandrian poet, C. P. Cavafy. One in particular, *The Mirror in the Hall,* is a telling verbal counterpart to this deceptively simple painting.

*Peter. C* 1961
David Hockney (born 1937)
Oil on canvas, 111.5 x 40.5 cm

Purchased with the assistance of The Friends of Manchester City Galleries and the MGC / V&A Purchase Grant Fund

*Opposite:*

As Augustus John, her celebrated artist brother, predicted, Gwen John's fame has outstripped his own. Studying at the Slade, she then moved to Paris and enrolled at the Académie Julian. She studied under Whistler, settled in France in 1904 and became the model and lover of the sculptor Rodin.

A committed individualist, her unique body of work is grounded upon her frankness and humility before her chosen subject matter. The result of quiet, sustained observation and infused with a supremely lyrical intensity, her paintings achieve a complete fusion of perception and the expressive possibilities of her chosen medium of paint. This painting shows her characteristic use of a limited and distinctive range of colours – chalky browns, pinks, mauves and blues applied to the canvas to create an attractive, muted surface of broken tones that define the scene.

Her work is at once modest and monumental, simple but elusive, delicate yet strong. Like the poetry of Emily Dickinson, Gwen John's paintings are commonplace and extraordinary at the same time. The chosen subject is a typical one for the artist, in fact for many artists who wish to suggest a sense of quiet absorption, stillness and tranquillity. However, the evident passivity of the subject is modified by the artist's own sensibility. The quiet reticence that is so evidently part of the appeal of John's work suggests not the limpness of countless Victorian depictions of beautiful, passive young women reading, but the inner strength and character associated with Vermeer's depictions of women.

*The Letter* 1924
(also called *The Convalescent*)
Gwen John, 1876–1939
Oil on canvas, 41.1 x 33.2 cm
Gift of Charles Lambert Rutherston

*Peasant Girl in a Wood Gathering
Faggots* 1782
Thomas Gainsborough (1727–88)
Oil on canvas, 169 x 123 cm
Purchased with the assistance of the V&A
Purchase Grant Fund and the National Art
Collections Fund

Gainsborough's subject, a young and pretty peasant girl, is painted in a manner that is more often associated with the great aristocratic portraits with which the artist gained his reputation.

Following the practice of Van Dyck, whom the artist greatly admired, Gainsborough designed his pictures to be seen from a distance. An artist of great technical facility, he painted at an extraordinary speed in a dimly lit studio that allowed him to block out the essentials of a picture without being distracted by details. With a few deft brushstrokes, painted wet on wet using long-handled brushes that were sometimes six foot in length, he swept in delicate veils of diluted paint which, when seen close, seem to dissolve into a sumptuous surface of iridescent colour. Once the basic composition was established he would use more conventionally made brushes to touch in the details, preserving the mood of the picture and the silvery tonality that is one of the hallmarks of his work. His contemporary and arch rival, Sir Joshua Reynolds, wrote admiringly of Gainsborough's skill: 'All those odd scratches and marks ... which even to experienced painters appear the effect of accident rather than design ... this shapeless appearance, by a kind of magick at a certain distance assumes form, and all the parts seem to drop into their proper places.'

This was painted in Gainsborough's final years when, tired of painting fashionable portraits, he turned his attention to what Reynolds called his 'pictures of fancy' – large-scale works on subjects of his own choice.

The street depicted is the rue de Voisins in Louveciennes, then a small village south west of Paris. With a patchwork of variegated dabs of paint, Pissarro has captured the precise effects of the low sun casting elongated shadows on an autumn day. The painting was produced very much with a Parisian audience in mind. Pissarro has presented not the glitzy flash of the new urban reality of Paris that attracted his associates Manet, Degas, Monet and Renoir, but *la France profonde*, the mythic image of unchanging rural existence that suggested a moral integrity not to be found in the modern city.

This is one of Pissarro's greatest works. The artist's modesty, sympathy and sincerity, his sensibility to tone and structure and his dedication to working through the problems of painting made him a respected and much-loved figure in his lifetime. Emile Zola, a critic, writer and early supporter of Impressionism, wrote that his paintings are '... the act of an honest man'. Cézanne memorably described his friend and mentor, 'the humble, colossal Pissarro'.

This painting is closely related to the work of Corot and also shows the influence of Monet. Pissarro liked to use a relatively restricted palette of ochres, blues and lilac greys in order to create a considered distribution of carefully related tones. This quiet street is suffused in a delicate, palpable light that caresses and defines the forms that are laid out in gentle pictorial harmony. The painting was bought in the 1870s and was one of the first Impressionist paintings to enter a British private collection.

*A Village Street, Louveciennes* 1871
Camille Pissarro (1831–1903)
Oil on canvas, 46 x 55.5 cm
Purchased with the assistance of the V&A
Purchase Grant Fund

*A 1944 Pastoral: Land Girls Pruning
at East Malling* 1944
Evelyn Dunbar (1906–60)
Oil on canvas, 91.3 x 121 cm
Gift of the War Artists Advisory Committee

Evelyn Dunbar was one of a number of artists commissioned during the Second World War to record the activities of the British people working together at a time of great national danger. In Dunbar's painting one can sense the exact character of the weather, almost smell the autumn and feel the blustery wind that blows through the leafless trees. While the men are absent at war, the volunteer women are pruning the fruit trees and preparing for the onset of winter and the following spring. This is part of the European tradition of painting the round of the seasons, showing how hard work ensures the production of food – a process often taken for granted today.

The gloved hands, saws, pruning shears and apples, placed around the outside edge of the canvas and which on occasion intrude upon the main image, create a dynamic interaction between the painted border and the composition it contains. The main image, its subject and the objects painted around it suggest not only an illustration from a handbook concerning the practicalities of agricultural activities, but also evoke the symbols (for example, trees, ladders and shawled women) associated with early Renaissance images of Christ's Passion. This lends to the ordinary scene a greater resonance than might be expected. Its evocation of community and place, its rather dry touch and quirky composition parallel the contemporary work of Spencer and Nash.

This teapot, modelled in the form of a startlingly life-like cockerel, is as inventive as a Picasso or Miro. It was probably modelled by the prolific and mysterious Johann Joachim Kaendler. He had worked at Meissen Porcelain Works since 1731, and one of his first commissions was to produce large-scale animal sculptures for Augustus the Strong's Japanese Palace. He was one of the most famous sculptors associated with Meissen and was largely responsible for introducing a more 'sculptural' quality into their ware.

This is one of a number of similar items that were produced at the factory at this time. Earlier examples owe much to the imported models from China which were in Augustus the Strong's collection, and similar teapots were made in 16th-century Istanbul. None, however, have the vitality of this wide-eyed fowl, with its feathers so beautifully captured by brushwork that is both free and precise.

Not only is this a supremely decorative object, but it is also functional. It could be the very model that Kaendler referred to in his work papers of May 1734: '... another teapot made in the shape of a cockerel of medium size, the tea pours from the spout in the same way. The tail is so constructed that it is possible to lift the cockerel high enough to pour from it.'

**Teapot** 1730–40
Attributed to Johann Joachim Kaendler
(1706–75)
Manufacturer: Meissen Porcelain Works
Hard-paste porcelain, painted overglaze.
Height: 19.9 cm

This dinner service was part of an adventurous but ultimately unsuccessful initiative to raise the standard of British design and to encourage the involvement of artists in the commercial world. A. J. Wilkinson Ltd was one of the three companies responsible for the project, despite the misgivings felt by its art director, the famous designer Clarice Cliff. A number of eminent artists, including Duncan Grant and Vanessa Bell, were commissioned to produce designs but it was generally agreed that most of the resulting pieces were disappointing. It proved impractical to translate the designs into mass production pieces, and the colours and patterns did not work within the context of the three-dimensional object.

However, this dinner service was an exception. Laura Knight's design uses the shapes of the service to great advantage, resulting in a piece of charm and invention. The handles are in the form of clowns, and the rims become the audience looking into the centre of the plates where, painted in Knight's distinctive style, the performers can be seen.

Born in Derbyshire, she was a successful and prolific artist. In 1936 she became one of the first female members of the Royal Academy.

The work of the artists involved in the project was shown to the public at Harrods in 1934, from which this service was bought for £70 by the popular Lancashire entertainer, Gracie Fields.

**Circus Dinner Service**, designed 1934
Dame Laura Knight (1877–1970)
Manufactured by A. J. Wilkinson Ltd,
1936
Earthenware, printed and painted
overglaze

Purchased with the assistance of The Friends
and the Corporate Patrons of Manchester City
Galleries, the MGC / V&A Purchase Grant Fund
and the National Art Collections Fund

*An Island* 1942
L. S. Lowry (1887–1976)
Oil on canvas, 45.6 x 60.9 cm

Lowry is Manchester's most famous painter and this image represents a lesser known aspect of his work but one that fascinated and troubled him. An inveterate wanderer about the land and townscapes of the industrial north, he would often tell of how he would inevitably gravitate towards the poorer quarters of wherever he happened to be, finding himself standing, fascinated, outside ruined or deserted houses. It is an image redolent of the Gothic imagination – such a strong element in British art and literature of the last two hundred years. He painted many different versions of this particular image; sometimes focusing upon a single house, sometimes depicting a broader scan of human habitation in which the centres of industry, government and worship are shown slipping into dissolution. In such pictures the boundaries between reality and fantasy, the external world and our own perception and understanding of it, are conveyed in simple, resonant images that refuse to offer any easy resolution.

Lowry represents not so much what is without, as what is within: he projected his own imaginative existence upon the real world that he inhabited. His paintings are a haunting series of symbolic structures that, once seen, are rarely forgotten. It is this ambivalence between the familiar and unfamiliar, the hint of the inexplicable, that is at the root of the effectiveness and popularity of Lowry's work.

Valette came to England from France in 1904 in the hope of finding employment in the cotton industry as a designer of printed fabrics. However, the exceptional nature of his draughtsmanship, firmly in the tradition of the great 19th-century French master Ingres, won him a teaching position at the Manchester School of Art where he remained until 1920, before returning to France in 1928.

For a number of years he created a series of impressive interpretations of Manchester, working in a manner that reflected his knowledge of Monet and Whistler. He seems to have taken to heart their concern with the artist's responsibility to create something exquisite and beautiful out of the ordinariness, and even vulgarity, of reality. The setting is instantly recognisable – the Albert Memorial and the smog-shrouded buildings that flank the square and Town Hall make a perfect foil for the figures. To the right of the composition, William Gladstone stands upon his plinth, arm raised, grasping a parliamentary bill as if trying to attract the attention of some nearby cabby.

The painting is characterised by its soft moody atmosphere, its simple and rigorous ordering of horizontals and verticals and its muted, limited palette. The eye is led from foreground to background through a series of subtly modulated tones. Such techniques, and the fact that Valette chose Manchester as the theme of his art, were matters not lost on L.S. Lowry, then an aspirant artist and a regular attender at Valette's life-drawing sessions. Lowry clearly learnt much from his teacher.

*Albert Square, Manchester* 1910
Adolphe Valette (1876–1942)
Oil on jute, 152 x 114 cm

In this piece, the victim lies upon a stretcher at the centre of a group of onlookers who react to the unexpected act of aggression according to their circumstances and character. How do we depict the flood of changing emotions that we feel and register instinctively in our expressions and gestures? This idea has been and remains one of the central concerns of Western culture.

Raymond Mason's work is forthright, almost ugly, in its directness. He revels in the bright colours of everyday clothing, the incidental details of ordinary life. Although it relates to the traditional Christian image of the dead Christ being taken down from the cross – so familiar a theme in European sculpture and painting – this image succeeds precisely because we don't know the circumstances of this person's death.

*L'Agression au 48 de la rue de Monsieur-le-Prince, Le 23 Juin 1975*
1976
Raymond Mason (born 1922)
Fibreglass. Height 54 cm
Purchased with the assistance of The Friends and Corporate Patrons of Manchester Art Galleries, the MGC / V&A Purchase Grant Fund and the Henry Moore Foundation

*Above:*

**The Courtyard of the Castle of
Königstein from the West** c.1756–58
Bernardo Bellotto (1720–80)
Oil on canvas, 133.9 x 238 cm

Purchased with the assistance of the V&A
Purchase Grant Fund, the National Heritage
Memorial Fund, the National Art Collections
Fund, the Corporate Patrons and The Friends of
Manchester City Galleries

*Left:*

**The Courtyard of the Castle of
Königstein from the South** c.1756–58
Bernardo Bellotto (1720–80)
Oil on canvas, 133.9 x 238 cm

Following the practice of his celebrated uncle, Canaletto, under whom he studied in Venice, it is possible that Bellotto used a 'camera obscura' to record the effects of perspective and tonal gradations that would have helped him make this image look so photographically exact.

Bellotto left his native Venice, perhaps because the prospect of trying to work in competition with his uncle was simply too daunting, and travelled to Rome before settling in Dresden to work for Frederick Augustus II of Saxony who appointed him court painter. He remained at court until 1758, producing many impressive panoramic views of the city. Later, he went to work for the Empress Maria Theresa in Vienna, eventually settling in Warsaw where he remained until his death.

Manchester owns two of the five views Bellotto produced of the Castle of Königstein in Saxony for Frederick Augustus, but the invasion of Augustus' territories by the Prussian army in 1756 meant that they were never delivered. In 1788, they were sold at Christie's and bought by the Marquis of Londonderry, from whom this picture and its partner were acquired.

The castle still stands on top of a rocky promontory surrounded by a ring of fortifications. At its centre was a walled garden with distinctive topiary, visible in this painting. Bellotto's style is characterised by a cool luminosity and a feeling for the incidental detail that owes much to his appreciation of Dutch 17th-century art.

An image of apocalyptic power, this is a potent reinvention, subversion even, of the British pastoral tradition of picturing the landscape. There is something deeply disturbing in the way that Middleditch has depicted the powerful and ever-moving presence of the rushing water on the static surface of this painting. Highly stylised, the pouring cataracts are shown like a central knot of twisting iron girders whilst the city huddles above the weir, etched against the nocturnal sky. This creates a powerful image of the disjunction between the forces of nature and those determined by man. The elemental force that spills over the man-made barriers of the weir is an effective metaphor for containment and release.

Middleditch specialised in simple but forceful compositions, often using only burnt umber, ochre, black and white in his work. Having served in the Second World War, he began his career comparatively late, studying at the Royal College of Art. His work sits well with that of Bomberg, Lowry and those artists associated with the return to realism which, for a brief period in the early 1950s, seemed to be the way ahead for British art.

*Sheffield Weir* c.1955
Edward Middleditch (1923–86)
Oil on hardboard, 122.2 x 152 cm

*La Ville Petrifiée (Petrified City)* 1933
Max Ernst (1891–1976)
Oil on paper stuck down on board,
50.5 x 60.9 cm

Max Ernst invented a number of techniques to stimulate his imagination. Rubbing a paint-covered piece of paper over a raised surface, he would stare intently at the result until an image suggested itself. He would then scrape the unwanted paint from the paper or canvas to free that image, adding touches of paint to bring into focus what had been prompted by his imaginative interpretation of the abstract forms to create a perfect synthesis of the conscious and unconscious.

Like Turner, he was interested in the fragility of human achievement in the face of the overwhelming might of nature. This work is one of a series he produced of strange settlements, reminiscent of abandoned jungle cities returned back to the vegetation. Directly related to the worsening situation in Europe at that time, his apocalyptic vision is paralleled in the work of Breughel and other European masters, as well as in the work of contemporary novelists such as J. G. Ballard and Manchester's Jeff Noon.

This artist chooses the titles for her pictures with care. 'Zephyr' is derived from the name of the Greek deity Zephyrus, the personification of the warm wind that brings life after winter. Invisible, it is only evident in the effect it has – the rustle of leaves in a tree or the ripples across the surface of an open stretch of water. When viewed, this cool, elegant painting triggers a retinal response from the viewer, as if the eye was responding to the stimulus before it like an ear might respond to a piece of music.

The immaculately painted surface, covered with a calculated order of chosen colours, begins to oscillate before our eyes with a gentle rhythm that suggests a continuous rippling movement. Too close a scrutiny, however, and the canvas freezes; relax and suddenly it springs back into movement, its undulating rhythms of form and colour being infinitely suggestive. As the French Symbolist poet, Mallarmé wrote, 'Paint not the thing, but the effect it produces.'

Many of the artist's canvases are intimately associated with her childhood memories of Cornwall. Her 'love of the seas, skies, bosky woods and secretive valleys ... what I experienced then,' she has said, 'was the basis of my visual life.' However, as Bridget Riley has suggested elsewhere, paintings such as this one should not be seen as illustrations of her own biography but as an attempt to provoke, '... the recognition of the sensation without the actual incident which prompted it.'

*Zephyr* 1976
Bridget Riley (born 1931)
Acrylic on linen, 225.4 x 107.3 cm
Purchased with the assistance of the Wilfred
R. Wood Bequest Fund

A painter turned potter, Cooper was introduced to ceramics by an Icelandic sculptor friend. He travelled to Iceland and was profoundly affected by the particular qualities of its rugged, highly textured landscape – qualities that he introduced into his pottery. He returned to England in 1950 where he moved to the seaside village of Porlock in Somerset. There he experimented with various rough stoneware bodies and wood ash glazes. He wrote of his fascination with 'the contrast of glazed and unglazed surfaces – an interest which has inspired all the work that I have done since.'

A bowl such as this one represents a break in the English studio pottery traditions dominated by the influence of Bernard Leach, whom Cooper admired but did not wish to imitate. The pattern work was created by it having been fired slowly over a period of up to several weeks, smouldering in the smoke of carefully chosen types of wood. Cooper would cut directly into the body of the piece, which he then rubbed with raw oxide so that the lines were highlighted. Iron gives a brown effect to the pot, whilst the application of manganese is responsible for the rich black of the lines.

In an age of mass production and high technology, craft pottery represents a human activity that stretches back to the earliest days of mankind and celebrates our interaction with the natural resources of earth, water, wood, air and fire to make objects necessary for our existence. Such pieces demand to be held. However, even situated in a gallery where they are unable to be handled, they can inspire the imagination of the viewer and reinvigorate aesthetic ambitions.

**Bowl** 1956
Waistel Cooper (born 1921)
Stoneware, incised and inlaid with manganese oxide, wood ash glaze to exterior. Height 21.7 cm

Central to the religious beliefs of the Egyptians was the need to preserve the body after death so that it could enjoy a full afterlife. In order to do so, a method of artificial preservation was developed, a process that could take up to 70 days to complete. The heart, the seat of the soul, was left within the body but the brain, regarded as useless, was discarded. The other internal organs had to be removed as quickly as possible and preserved. They were placed in four funeral or 'canopic' jars, of which this piece is an example.

The jars were made from a variety of materials and were specifically dedicated to, and protected by, one of the four sons of Horus, born of Isis. The jar containing the liver was set under the protection of human-headed Imset; the jar for the deceased's stomach was protected by jackal-headed Duamutef; and that holding the intestines was looked over by falcon-headed Qebehsenuf. The one containing the lungs had Hapi as a patron, who was personified as a baboon or dog. The jars were normally placed together but kept separate from the mummified body. If stolen, it was believed that the mummified viscera could be used to cast evil spells.

**Funeral Jar**
Egyptian (1567–1085 BC)
Alabaster. Height: 43.1 cm
Bequest of John E. Yates

This figure on horseback probably formed part of a symbolic retinue that would accompany the body to the grave. The number and variety of such pieces would relate directly to the wealth and status of the deceased. Each piece was meant to provide for the needs of the deceased in the afterlife. They would often be displayed outside the entrance of the tomb, to be subsequently taken inside and sealed up with the body. Since it was believed that death was the continuation of an earthly existence in another form, these figures represent the needs and activities of this world, and hence give a lively sense of how life was lived in the Tang dynasty. The Tang period was one of peace, when the country was secure and the arts flourished.

The figurine represents a female rider wearing men's clothes, as was customary at the time. An old treatise on carriages and dress records how, 'Highborn or lowborn men and women, could not be distinguished from one another, all looked alike'. Owning a fine horse symbolised wealth and influence, as did the number of chariots a person owned, and also the significant attributes of energy, harmony and grace.

The horse and rider are made from grey earthenware, hollow-moulded in separate parts, luted together and then glued with dilute clay. The horse is covered by a white slip, with a painted black bridle. The livery is highly detailed, the pendants in the form of lobed cusps hold red roundels which hang from the front and rear saddle straps. Swirling scrolls of yellow ochre decorate the large round saddle cloth, picked out in red and black, and the beautifully poised rider wears a long, narrow-sleeved coat painted red, with a V-shaped opening at the neck turned back to reveal an ochre lining. The features of the face are clearly discernible as is her elaborate hairstyle.

**Tomb Figure** c. AD 706
High Tang period, China (AD 618–907)
Earthenware painted in unfired colours. Height: 38 cm

This is a rare surviving example of a Tudor beaker complete with its cover. In this period this type of cup was referred to in wills and inventories as a 'Magdalen' or 'Mawdyln' cup, which is a reference to the cup carried by Mary Magdalen. According to St Luke's Gospel (Luke, 7: 37), she was 'a woman in the city' who was 'a sinner', who came to Jesus as he ate at the house of a Pharisee bearing a pot of ointment. She washed Christ's feet with her tears and dried them with her hair, anointing them with the balm she had brought.

The cup's cylindrical body is decorated with fantastical grotesques, derived from antique wall painting and revived during the Renaissance period by Raphael. Winged cherub-heads hover over vases laden with fruit, whilst birds, monstrous creatures, animals' heads and meandering snails complete this fantastical extravaganza. The outer surface of the cover is decorated with richly embossed *repoussé* swags, whilst the underside of the cover carries at its centre a finely engraved Tudor rose.

**The Magdalen Cup** 1573–74
Silver gilt, maker's mark 'M H' in monogram. Height 19.3 cm

*Opposite:*

Painted by an artist working in the circle of Duccio, one of the greatest artists of the period, this is an image of separation, suffering and sacrifice. It depicts the precise moment of Christ's death high above the assembled crowd, each of whom react to the event according to their nature. His mother, dressed in dark blue, turns away and is supported by her friends as she collapses in grief. To the other side of her, St John looks on, whilst behind him, echoing the raised lances of the soldiery, Mary Magdalen lifts her open arms in useless supplication. On the right-hand side of the panel are the scribes and Pharisees, and a man throwing dice for the seamless robe of Christ. Amongst them is the centurion who, at the instant of Christ's death, realises the awesome significance of the event.

The scene merges the symbolic and actual into one convincing whole. The expressions and gestures all powerfully convey shared human experience. The blood of Christ drips down from the point of the raised lance, falling into the eyes of its bearer and onto the earth. At the foot of the cross the ground opens and Christ's blood settles on the skull of Adam, a symbolic declaration of the beginning of mankind's redemption through Christ's sacrifice. The gold of the background is designed to suggest to a believer in Catholic doctrine that Christ's sacrifice was not just a historic moment in time, but one that eternally recurs in the act of receiving Holy Communion.

*The Crucifixion* c.1330
Follower of Duccio (c.1255–1319?)
Egg tempera on panel with gold ground,
59.7 x 38 cm

Purchased with the assistance of the National Art
Collections Fund, John Paul Getty II, the Henry
Moore Foundation, the National Heritage Memorial
Fund, the V&A Purchase Grant Fund, the Pilgrim
Trust, the Corporate Patrons and The Friends of
Manchester City Galleries and private donations

Western art abounds in images of the human body, indicating a need to produce images of ourselves, our anxieties, desires, fears, beliefs, frailties and mortality. This painting makes a fitting endpiece. It is a memorial to Sir Thomas Aston's wife, a reminder of our own mortality and the ability of art to transcend time itself – at once an image of loss and remembrance. Sir Thomas' son points to a cross held by his fashionably dressed father, who stands slightly off balance between the images of life and death. Sir Thomas' hand rests on a skull set upon a cradle wrapped in black cloth, suggesting that his wife died in childbirth. The figure inclining her head in the traditional gesture of melancholia is believed to be his dead wife as she was in life.

The continuity of the family is registered by the prominent heraldic shield. Death conquers all, a knowledge that must be stoically endured, and only memory allows us a pale victory against the inevitability of death, although the Latin texts situated about the painting make a resolute declaration of faith in eternal life. Like so many others reproduced in this book, this painting stands as an example of our need to question and understand the spaces between representation and reality.

*Sir Thomas Aston at the Deathbed of his Wife* 1635
John Souch (active 1616–36)
Oil on canvas, 203.2 x 215.1 cm
Gift of Peter Jones through the National Art Collections Fund

## Acknowledgements

*Up Close* has been created with the assistance of many staff at Manchester City Galleries, in particular Howard Smith (Head of Curatorial Services), who initiated and devised the book with Michael Howard, and Ruth Greenbaum (Commercial Officer). Photography was by Alan Seabright and Richard Weltman. Howard Smith acknowledges the important contribution made by his colleagues in the Conservation Section in preparing works of art for photography and display, and also those in the Collections Management Section responsible for their documentation and subsequent installation in the galleries. The author thanks the Decorative Art and Fine Art staff for their help in preparing this book. Finally, Michael Howard and Howard Smith would like to thank the team at Scala Publishers, especially Miranda Harrison (Editorial Director) and Yvonne Dedman (book designer), for guiding the book through publication with patience and professionalism.

## Copyright Credits

*Right:*
**An Island** (detail) 1942,
by L.S. Lowry (see page 72)